Hedieh Najafi has a Ph.D. in Educational Leadership and Policy Studies and an M.A. in English Literature. After years teaching in institutions of higher education in different countries around the world and writing scholarly articles, she is now taking some time to focus on writing creatively. Her poem *"Strange Fruit Perpetuates"* was published in the 11th issue of the literary magazine, Dryland, in September 2021.

FOOD FOOD FOOD ALL IS GOOD

Hedieh Najafi

AUSTIN MACAULEY PUBLISHERS™

LONDON • CAMBRIDGE • NEW YORK • SHARJAH

To my husband, the love of my life, who always believed in me and encouraged me.
Without him this work would have never been published.

I would like to thank my parents, husband, and two daughters for their incessant
support and love.

Food, food, food

All is good
I love fast food
I love slow food
I love hot food
I love cold food.

I eat carrots
But not parrots
I eat corns
But not horns.

I shake and bake
I brew what I grew
I thrill when I grill
But I cry when I fry.

I love apples
Red apples and pineapples
Apples of the mainland
Thailand and the island
But not those in the la la land!

Junk food sickens
I don't say dickens
Junk food thickens
It also weakens.

I love macaroni
With baloney and broccoli
I love spaghetti
Spinach in ravioli.

I love protein
Vitamin and carotene
And everything in between
All kinds of cuisine.

I love Lebanese food
Chinese and Cantonese food
I love Taiwanese food
Japanese and Sudanese food.

I eat carrots in cakes
Crabs in cakes
And fish in lakes
This is all it takes.

I like all kinds of cakes
Carrot cakes, corn cakes, and moon cakes
Whatever that bakes
For goodness' sake.

I eat rice
I eat white rice
I eat brown rice
But not dice and rice.

I love couscous
I love chocolate mousse
I love couscous and Dr. Seuss
But not Dr. Seuss in chocolate mousse.

I love soups
Soups in groups
Tomato soups and potato soups
Don't forget those chicken soups.

I love mushrooms in hot rooms
I love mushrooms in cold rooms
But not the mushrooms on the grooms
Or the mushrooms on the brooms.

Sometimes...
I eat chips, all kinds of chips
I eat potato chips, carrot chips,
And chocolate chips
But never computer chips.

I eat fish
Not the blue and red fish
Not the Dr. Seuss' fish
But the fish on a dish.

Vermicelli in a fish
Rice and raisins in a fish
Herbs but not nerds in a fish.

I love fruit
Sea fruit,
And the dragon fruit,
Don't forget that star fruit.

ORLANDO
BEACH

I love the mango
From the Congo
I eat a mango
When in Orlando.

I love corn beef but not cold beef
I love hot beef but not raw beef
I love roast beef but not soft beef
I love beef on a green leaf!

I love fruit kabab and shish kabab
I love kabab
I love rhubarb
But not rhubarb in the kabab.

I love peas, snow peas
Green peas and
Snap peas
Even hummus with chickpeas.

I love cheese, Gouda cheese and Feta cheese
Bread and cheese
Grapes and cheese
Don't forget those beans on cheese.

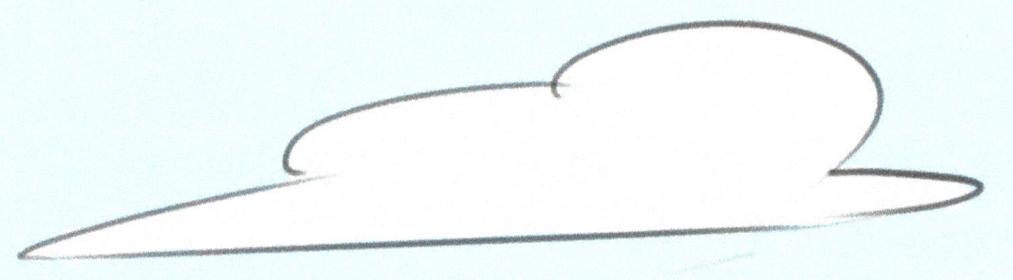

I love nuts
Walnuts and peanuts
But if you can't have nuts
Just have some coconuts.

I eat Tahini
But not bikini
I eat calamari
But not safari.

*Food, food, food
All is good!*

THE
END